When I am happy

Bobbie Kalman

 Crabtree Publishing Company

www.crabtreebooks.com

Created by Bobbie Kalman

Author and
Editor-in-Chief
Bobbie Kalman

Reading consultant
Elaine Hurst

Editors
Kathy Middleton
Crystal Sikkens
Joan King

Special thanks to
Jennifer King, Educational consultant

Design
Bobbie Kalman
Katherine Berti

Photo research
Bobbie Kalman

Production coordinator
and Prepress technician
Katherine Berti

Photographs by Shutterstock

Library and Archives Canada Cataloguing in Publication

Kalman, Bobbie, 1947-
    When I am happy / Bobbie Kalman.

(My world)
ISBN 978-0-7787-9503-2 (bound).--ISBN 978-0-7787-9528-5 (pbk.)

    1. Happiness--Juvenile literature. I. Title. II. Series: My
world (St. Catharines, Ont.)

BF723.H37K34 2011   j152.4'2   C2010-901971-7

Library of Congress Cataloging-in-Publication Data

Kalman, Bobbie.
    When I am happy / Bobbie Kalman.
        p. cm. -- (My world)
    ISBN 978-0-7787-9528-5 (pbk. : alk. paper) -- ISBN 978-0-7787-9503-2
(reinforced library binding : alk. paper)
    1. Happiness--Juvenile literature. 2. Happiness in children--Juvenile
literature. I. Title. II. Series.

    BF723.H37K35 2011
    152.4'2--dc22
                                                                    2010011298

Crabtree Publishing Company

www.crabtreebooks.com   1-800-387-7650

Printed in Hong Kong/042011/BK20110304

Published in Canada
Crabtree Publishing
616 Welland Ave.
St. Catharines, Ontario
L2M 5V6

Published in the United States
Crabtree Publishing
PMB 59051
350 Fifth Avenue, 59th Floor
New York, New York 10118

Published in the United Kingdom
Crabtree Publishing
Maritime House
Basin Road North, Hove
BN41 1WR

Published in Australia
Crabtree Publishing
386 Mt. Alexander Rd.
Ascot Vale (Melbourne)
VIC 3032

Words to know

bake   clap   clown   dance (tap)

draw   hug   jump (shout)   kiss   laugh

play (friends)   read   smile

3

I **smile** when I am happy.
I like to smile.

I **laugh** when I am happy.
I like to laugh.

I **clap** my hands when I am happy.
I like to clap.

I **tap** my feet when I am happy.
I like to tap-**dance**.

I **hug** my brother when I am happy.
I say to him, "I like you."

brother

I **kiss** my mom when I am happy.
I say, "I love you, Mom."

I act funny when I am happy.
My **friends** say, "You are a **clown**."

I **jump** and **shout**
when I am happy.
I shout, "I am happy!"

I am happy when I **read** a book.
I like to read funny stories.

I am happy when I **bake** cookies.
I say, "Mmm, I like cookies."

What makes you happy?

Are you happy
when you **play**?

Are you happy
when you hug
your friends?

Are you happy
when you **draw**?

What do you say
when you are happy?

Notes for adults

Objectives
- to learn how children show that they are happy
- to learn what makes children happy
- to explore what happiness is

Questions before reading the book
"How do you show that you are happy?"
"What makes you happy?"
"Where do you feel the most happy?"
"With which people do you feel happiest?"
"How does being happy feel?"

Questions after reading the book
"Which of these actions show that you are happy?" (clapping hands, smiling, tapping feet, hugging, kissing, acting funny, jumping and shouting)
"Which things make you happy?" (reading a book, baking cookies, playing, hugging friends, drawing pictures)
"What do you say when you are happy? Do you tell people you like them?"
"Do you give compliments to others so that they will feel happy, too?"

Activity: Turn it around
Say each sentence in the book out loud and ask the children to turn it around. For example: "I smile when I am happy. I am happy when I smile."
"I laugh when I am happy. I am happy when I laugh."
Ask the children if they can tell the difference between the first sentence and the second. (The first indicates the body language of happiness, and the second shows the causes of happiness.)

Activity
Record the children talking about what makes them happy.
Ask them to design happy faces using different colored papers. Ask them to choose colors that make them feel happy. On each happy face, write one word that makes them happy or shows that they are happy. (smile, laugh, dance, leap, hug)

Extensions
Explore with the children the different states of happiness by setting up examples of the following: excitement, contentment, pride, having "alone" time, daydreaming, feeling good about helping others, having fun, anticipation of happy events, enjoyment, accomplishment, and the inner joy of feeling good about their lives.

For teacher's guide, go to www.crabtreebooks.com/teachersguides